Scott House Souvenirs

Scott House Souvenirs

James Sheetz  Marlene Wisuri

Dovetailed Press LLC
Duluth, Minnesota

Copyright © 2007 by James Sheetz and Marlene Wisuri

All rights reserved. No part of this book may be reproduced in any form, except short excerpts for review and educational purposes, without the written permission of the publisher.

ISBN 10 0-9765890-1-X
ISBN 13 978-0-9765890-1-3

Library of Congress Control Number 2007921884

Printed and bound in the United States of America
Book layout and design by Marlene Wisuri
Cover photographs by Marlene Wisuri

Dovetailed Press LLC
5263 North Shore Drive
Duluth, MN 55804
www.dovetailedpress.com

Dedications

to my parents, Doris M. and the late Donald R. Sheetz, for entrusting me with the legacy of Scott House

James Sheetz

to the memory of my brother, Wilfred Wisuri, Jr.

Marlene Wisuri

Doris and Don Sheetz, 2000.

Acknowledgements

We would like to thank everyone who helped make our community/family history and photography project come alive, including the Scott family, Susan Chapin, Roberta Malwitz, Larry Luukkonen, Millie Lee, and the late Wayne Swanson. We would especially like to thank the members of our families who assisted us with information, critiques, photographs, and their patient support.

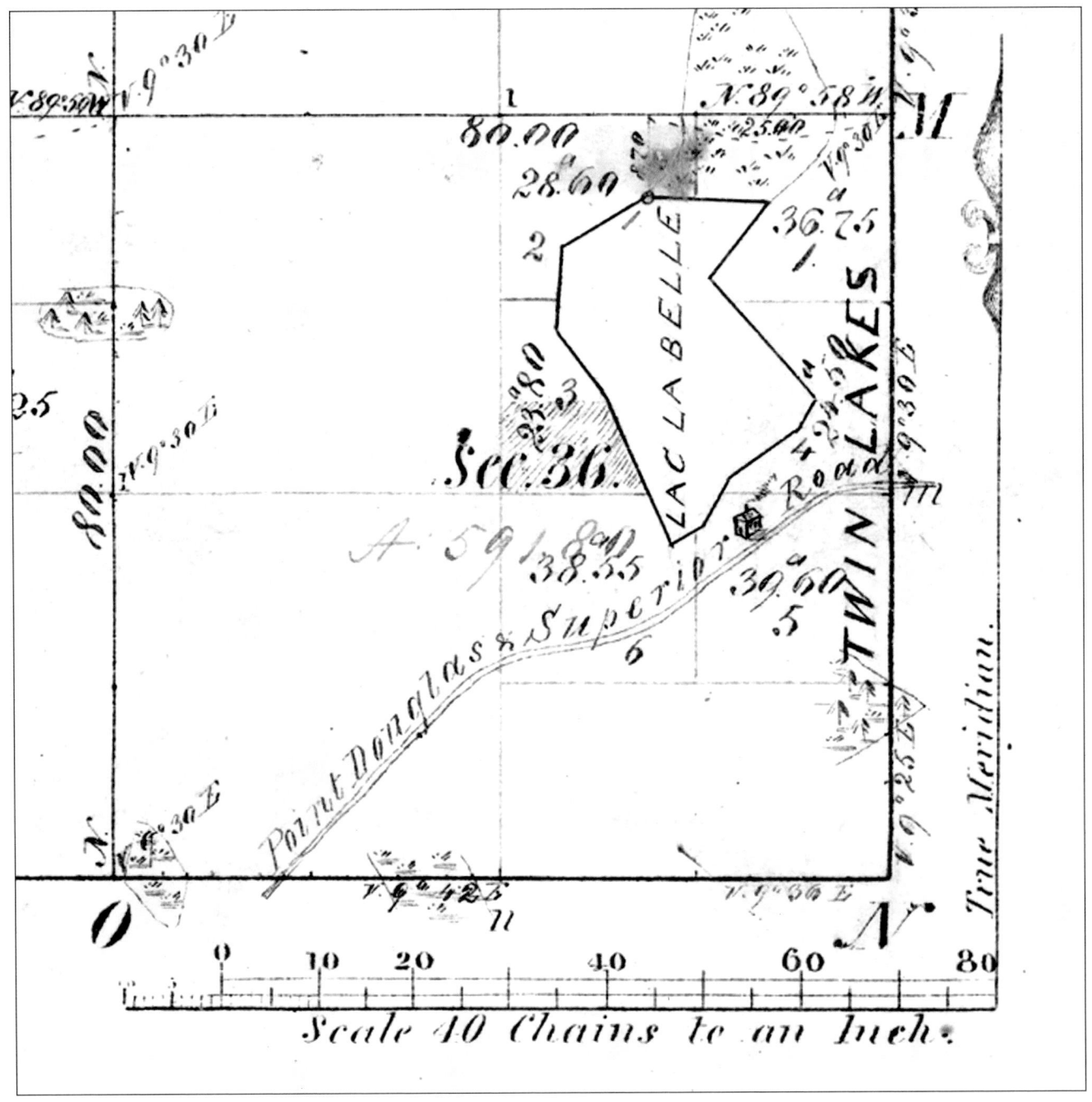

The Point Douglas to Superior Military Road and the location of the stage stop (the site of Scott House) are indicated on this detail from a Land Survey Map of 1861. The stage stop is noted with a little house symbol complete with smoke coming from the chimney.

Table of Contents

Introduction	8
Scott House Timeline & History	10
The Road Through the Wilderness	12
The Mayer Years	26
The Scotts of Scott's Corner	28
Minnie Scott's Letters	34
The Sheetz Family at Scott House	44
The Renovation of Scott House	52
Scott House Portfolio	58
Scott House Recipes	72
About the Authors	80

A fragment of the original barn at Scott House.

Introduction

Soon after assuming my position as Director of the Carlton County Historical Society, I began learning about the "old Military Road," which ran through Carlton County on its path from Point Douglas near St. Paul to Superior, Wisconsin in the 1850s and 60s. One of three stage stops on the road in Carlton County was located on Lac La Belle (at Twin Lakes), in what later became known as Scott House. An aura of adventure lingers in the thoughts of this primitive transportation system and equally primitive stopover place sheltered under towering pines. Although the current Scott House building served as a stage stop hotel for a relatively short time before the Military Road was superseded by the railroad in 1870, the location itself holds a place of historic importance as way station, county seat, and crossroads for a growing rural community.

I have watched the transformation of Scott House from a family residence to a renovated events center with interest. Having known James Sheetz for about a decade and a half, I have delighted in his "collecting nature," which apparently began when he was quite young. His extensive collections have served as focal points for the restoration of Scott House and the collections, period furniture, and the house itself provided me with subjects for the series of still life photographs you will find in this book.

I believe photographs to be rather magical objects that can only suggest the reality of the moment through combinations of light and dark and fleeting glances as life unfolds before us. In these images I have attempted to still those glances and present fragments of (still) life for contemplation and as things of beauty. Because of the historic nature of the building and the collections, it is tempting to view the images as merely nostalgic. I hope to transcend pure nostalgia with the realization of both the fragility of life and its enduring qualities, for in many cases the objects pictured have survived much longer than their original owners. In some of the collections there is a certain curiousness or quirkiness that has delighted me and with others there is a feeling of some sadness that comes with knowledge of the passage of time. I present the images both as historic documents and objects of art.

In the text of the book, we have attempted to remain true to the voices of the people who occupied or have passed through Scott House. Whenever possible we have provided actual quotes or writings of the time. Jim has also provided a first person narrative you will find throughout the book. It is our hope that some of the feeling engendered by this special building in the past will be recreated in the readers of *Scott House Souvenirs*.

Marlene Wisuri

The idyllic setting, early origins, and history of Scott House have always had a particular fascination for me. Living there afforded me the opportunity of growing up in a place that welcomed weary travelers who had endured the difficulty of traveling by stage coach on rough roads through the vast and untouched wilds of Northern Minnesota. I was also fortunate in my "growing up" years to have known some of the pioneers who shared their early memories of Scott House—memories I collected.

Scott House is a modest, plainly constructed building, fashioned of materials which came from the property itself. Within these sturdy walls there is a history of community, family, guests, and travelers that has existed for nearly 140 years.

During my term as President of the Carlton County Historical Society, the desire to renovate Scott House into an events center was encouraged by Marlene Wisuri. The images she has created for this book have not only stirred in me fond memories of a by-gone era, but also provided the opportunity to share the enduring beauty of the past.

I hope you will enjoy this brush with history.

James Sheetz

Scott House Timeline & History

1851 ~ The Point Douglas to St. Louis River Military Road is surveyed and construction begins on the road which continues for several years. Twin Lakes serves as a stage stop on the road.

1854 ~ The terminus of the Military Road is changed from the rapids of the St. Louis River to Superior, Wisconsin.

1857-1870 ~ The station at Twin Lakes serves as the county seat for Carlton County until its relocation to Thomson after the opening of the Lake Superior & Mississippi Railroad in 1870.

January, 1862 ~ Property is purchased by Chester Williams by patent from the United States Government.

Late 1860s ~ A frame building is designed and built, probably by Chester Williams, to be used as an inn on the Point Douglas to Superior Military Road. An early source states, "stage coach passengers enjoyed the genial hospitality of their host, Chester Williams."

1881-1909 ~ The Joseph and Rebecca Mayer family own the property and farm the land.

1910-1937 ~ The Walter and Minnie Scott family reside on the property and farm.

1912 ~ Plumbing and an upstairs bathroom are installed by Walter Scott using water from Lac La Belle.

1914 ~ Walter and Minnie Scott are divorced. Minnie is awarded the land, household, and farm possessions.

1937 ~ Minnie Scott dies in Wausau, Wisconsin, where she had gone to live with her son Russell. Minnie's personal property is removed from Scott House and sold at auction in the spring of 1937.

1940 ~ Harry and Rowena Sheetz rent Scott House from John Duffy.

1942 ~ Property is sold to Harry Sheetz who remodels the large old fashioned kitchen by removing a back stairway and pantry and covering the ornamental tin ceiling.

1948 ~ New plumbing is installed.

1949 ~ Don and Doris Sheetz purchase the property for $3,000.00.

1949-2000 ~ Don and Doris Sheetz live in Scott House and raise a family of two sons and two daughters.

1950s ~ Various remodeling projects are completed including window replacement, lowering of downstairs ceilings, moving the front stairwell, kitchen renovation, and roof and siding repair.

Spring, 2000 ~ Don and Doris Sheetz move to a new home on Lac La Belle. James Sheetz begins the renovation of Scott House.

June 5, 2000 ~ The Carlton County Historical Society holds a Carlton/Twin Lakes Party in the midst of the renovation activity.

September 7 & 8, 2001 ~ A Renovation Completion celebration is held.

2001-2007 ~ Scott House finds new life as an events center.

A Road Through the Wilderness

Imagine, if you will, the beauty of this northern land with its towering pine trees, groves of hardwoods, cedar swamps, and clear lakes. The land had been occupied for hundreds of years by indigenous people who practiced sustainable living using the abundance of wood products, game, fish, wild rice, fruits, and berries to provide food, clothing, and shelter. This way of life had changed with exploration, the fur trade, and a scattering of white settlers beginning about 1650. The next two centuries saw dramatic changes in the way land was viewed and distributed.

After the formation of Minnesota territory in 1848, public interest was growing in the building of roads to connect the riches of northern Minnesota and Wisconsin with the settlements springing up on the banks of the Mississippi and in the St. Croix River valley. Roads that would allow for the transport of goods, people, and mail were seen as vital to the continued settlement of the territory and the development of the lumber industry. Ostensibly there was also a need for means of troop transport in case of unrest among the Indian population. A valuable connection to the entire Great Lakes shipping system would also be made with the completion of the ship canal at Sault Sainte Marie, Michigan, in 1855.

The new territorial legislature, represented by Henry H. Sibley, appealed to the United States Congress for funds to build "military roads" throughout the territory. After a lengthy debate, the Minnesota Road Act was passed by Congress and became effective on July 18, 1850. It allowed for the appropriation of forty thousand dollars to be used for the construction of four roads and surveying of a fifth under the supervision of Colonel John J. Abert, chief of the War Department's Bureau of Topographical Engineers.

The first road, called the Point Douglas to St. Louis River Military Road, lead "from Point Douglas, on the Mississippi, via Cottage Grove, Stillwater, Marine Mills, and the falls of the St. Croix to the falls or rapids of the St. Louis River of Lake Superior" with $15,000 appropriated for its building. This road was the longest and most costly of the five proposed roads. The route was surveyed in 1851 by a civilian engineer—John S. Potter. A second survey was undertaken under the direction of 1st Lieutenant James H. Simpson, Corps of Topographical Engineers, who served as the superintendent of the military road building until May, 1856, when he was replaced by Captain George Thom. Thom served until May of 1858 when Captain Howard

Stansbury took over until the government road office was closed in 1861. In 1853, an additional $45,000 was appropriated for the construction of Minnesota military roads. Additional federal funds were appropriated by Congress in 1854-55 and 1857.

In January of 1854, impatient for the government road to be completed, residents of Superior took matters into their own hands and commenced hacking a "winter road" out of the wilderness from Superior to Chase's landing on the St. Croix River. This trail was constructed by seventeen volunteers from Superior and was thought to have been funded by businessmen from St. Paul who had an interest in commercial growth at the head of the lakes. George Nettleton, owner of a stage line in Superior, was reportedly instrumental in the building of the winter road. The winter road was later mostly abandoned in favor of the government financed and engineered military road, but its existence has caused confusion for historians ever since.

The original plan for the government military road to end at the falls of the St. Louis River was changed in July of 1854 when Congress designated a point opposite the mouth of the river in Superior, Wisconsin, as the northern terminus of the road. Political maneuvering and the prior existence of the "winter road" may have led to the change. The length of the road also changed as alterations were made in the route so that distances ranged from 178 to 185 miles. Road construction stretched over several years with 1855 being the most productive.

A government report declared the Military Road finally completed on April 30, 1858, although it never existed in a totally finished state. Actual construction of the road was done by civilian contractors from the St. Paul area and Superior under military supervision headed by 1st Lt. Simpson. Relays or way stations were designated at fourteen points on the road between Superior and St. Paul. The stations, located near lakes or rivers, provided services and supplies for travelers and their livestock.

The road reportedly opened for travel in late December 1855 or early January 1856. However, Carlisle Doble set out with a wagon load of passengers on December 12, 1855, only to find the road was not entirely passable. In November of 1857, Mr. Doble was awarded a contract to carry the mail three times a week between Superior and Taylor's Falls using six two-horse sleighs. Each run was estimated to take three and a half days.

Articles found in the *Superior Chronicle*, tell the story of the construction and the opening of the road. These accounts often contain predictions for thriving growth and prosperity in the region.

On June 12, 1855, the *Chronicle* reported:

This road, which is being built by the General Government, was surveyed in 1852, and is now making rapid progress toward completion. The distance was one hundred and eighty-eight miles by the original survey, but several changes made in this end of the route have shortened it about sixteen miles. A route has been lately surveyed from St. Paul intersecting with this road at the eighty-first mile stone, which is fifty-five miles from that place. By this connection, the distance from Superior to St. Paul will be one hundred and forty-seven miles.

The last appropriation is now being applied to the opening and bridging of the road, by efficient contractors—Mr. Ludden on the St. Croix and Mr. O. [Orrin] W. Rice on the Lake Superior end. With ordinary exertions, it is anticipated that a good wagon route will be opened by Christmas. The engineer has just returned from a reconnoissance of some twenty or twenty-five miles, and reports the ground, to the dividing ridge between the Lake and St. Croix waters, rising to an elevation of eight hundred feet. The land, he reports, is of excellent quality, timbered with sugar maple, lynn, elm, ash, and white oak, interspersed with groves of pine. Until now, the existence of this region of good land was not generally known, and within the last few days settlers have gone out to secure farms. When the first travelers come through, they will find this end of the road lined with settlements.

A letter written by A. S. Mitchell, a visitor to the area and editor of the *St. Louis Intelligeneer* to Mr. L. B. Crocker of Oswego, New York, was published in the *Chronicle* on August 7, 1855, and contains some overly optimistic predictions about the completion of the road:

It may be interesting to know that a Government wagon road is in the course of construction between Superior and St. Paul.—Two thirds of the distance have already been opened. By November, it is probable that horsemen, cattle, and perhaps small vehicles may be passing through. By the 15th of December the whole work is to be finished. A tri-weekly line of stages will at once commence running between Superior and the Mississippi river; and the adventurous, the practical and hardy pioneers, of the Mississippi Valley, who have become inured to the work of subduing the wilderness, will come pouring up, and filling the shore of Lake Superior and the forest and prairies stretching off to the west of it.

An account of the alternative route constructed by Superiorites prior to the completion of the Government or Military Road is explained in the August 21, 1855, *Superior Chronicle*:

> The route to Hudson is in common with that to St. Paul—as far as Stillwater. The first fifty miles to St. Croix River, is a cutout road, traveled in winter by teams, and in summer on foot only. It is known to most of our early settlers as the "St. Croix trail," on which many a wearied traveler has held a rejoicing as he neared its end. In winter and summer from there to St. Croix Falls we have a fine road over rolling prairie and open timbered land, but in navigable seasons the traveler usually takes a batteaux or canoe on the river to the falls—a very pleasant ride, abounding in bold and changing scenery....
>
> ...The route to St. Paul, via the Government road is yet but little known, except by the engineers and contractors. Twin Lakes, (Corchoran's station) twenty-one miles out, is said to be in the heart of an excellent region of land. The lakes are pure, clear water, sandy beach, and the fact that the land along the road is nearly all pre-empted from here to that point, and even beyond, induces the belief that this route, when finished, will be extensively traveled. The remaining seventy miles is now under contract to Messrs. O. W. Rice and Lugden, who, we are assured, will, without delay, press forward the work to completion in time for winter travel.

There were colorful descriptions of goods being transported over the Military Road around Christmas time in 1856 under the title *Overland Travel*:

> We understand that there are eight or ten teams, destined for Superior, on the military road between St. Paul and this place. Some have oysters and canned fruits, and others are loaded with venison. In return, we can send our neighbors some delicious lake fish. The exchange of these articles, with the passenger travel, will keep up quite a brisk intercourse between St. Paul and Superior.
> *Superior Chronicle*, December 16, 1856

And on December 23...

> Two teams arrived last evening, and report that there are ten or twelve more coming. They bring

us fresh pork, beef, venison, and bear meat. Several of our citizens have made purchases of goods and cattle, at St. Paul, amounting to upwards of six thousand dollars.

The January 6, 1857, *Chronicle* reflects on the past and looks optimistically toward the future:

Two years ago, a trip from St. Paul to Superior, was almost an inconceivable undertaking, Indian guides being required, devious paths to be followed, and weeks of hardship to be endured. Now, a magnificent wagon road cut by Government, costing over $100,000 unites St. Paul and Superior, and mingles the commerce and travel of Lake Superior and the Upper Mississippi. And during the approaching winter, stages loaded with people, and wagons loaded with stores, will daily be passing each other on the road between St. Paul and Superior.

The station at Twin Lakes not only served as a trading post and general store, but also as an inn for travelers. Between 1857 and 1870, it was also the county seat for Carlton County until the court house was relocated to Thomson after the opening of the Lake Superior & Mississippi Railroad in 1870. Chester Williams, John Dunphy, and "the genial" George Stull served as innkeepers at different times.

The *Superior Chronicle* of April 14, 1857, offered this description of Twin Lakes taken from an article from the *Pioneer and Democrat*:

Six miles beyond (Blackhoof) lies the town of "Twin Lakes," recently laid out, and made the county seat of Twin Lake county (sic). The land around this point is, perhaps, the best between Superior and Snake river, and full equal, we think, to any along the route. The proprietors of this town are eager in their hopes and anticipate its becoming in time quite an important point: and as in earnest of what is to come, any number of shares have been issued and sold already at quite high rates. These new towns are still in an embryo state, but another year will no doubt produce a wonderful change in their condition and appearance.

The article continues with a description of the road itself...

The government road to Superior for winter travel, is very good: from eighty to one hundred feet in width, well cleared and grated, and smooth for nearly the entire distance. Immense rows of heavy pines and birch, with their white waving tops, "like Harpars of old, with beards hoary and frosty," stand like guardians and sentinels on either side, affording a most perfect protection against the winds.

Another road called the Crow Wing-Lake Superior Territorial Road or the "Mille Lacs Road" was constructed to connect Crow Wing with Lake Superior by intersecting with the Military Road south of Twin Lakes. This territorial road provided an important connection with the Mississippi River system to the west.

Yet another route connected Twin Lakes to the city of Duluth. Minnesota legislation in 1858 funded a survey from Twin Lakes to Duluth via Fond du Lac and four years later appropriated five hundred dollars for a winter road between Twin Lakes and Duluth. Additional monies of a matching amount were to be provided by the counties. The road from Duluth to Twin Lakes was finished during the summer of 1869 not long before train service began in August, 1870.

Conditions of travel for the Military Road and accommodations of the stage stop at Twin Lakes are described in varying terms from glowing to disparaging in written accounts of the time. Years after the fact, Luke A. Marvin recounted the trip made by his parents from St. Paul to Superior in 1861:

It was a tradition in those early days that no woman could stand the trials of a journey over the old Government military road between St. Paul and Superior, and as far as I know my mother was the first woman to adventure it, although on this point I am not certain. (*Note: Mrs. Pete made the trip in February, 1856, six weeks before delivering a son in Superior. During the trip she almost lost her life when the wagon was upset and she was wedged between the wagon load and a tree.*) At any rate, she insisted on coming along with my father, saying that if he could stand the trip she guessed she could too. We were a week making the 150 miles or so that the road extended, and it certainly was a terrible trip. The whole distance lay through a dense forest, and through this forest the trees had been felled on a space wide enough for a road on which teams could pass each other. Stumps stuck up all over the road. In many places it was very marshy and trees had been cut down to make a corduroy. There were no springs to the coach, and we would go bumping over stumps, in momentary danger of upsetting at times; at others our wheels would be past the hubs in mud, out of which it would take the utmost power of the horses to pull us. At intervals along the road there were relay houses, where we could change horses, and where we would generally pass the nights. All the accommodations were of the roughest and most primitive kind.

Pictured above is a stagecoach similar to the type that was used on the Military Road. Harry Ashton described them in an early account:

> These stages were built at Concord, New Hampshire, and were generally known as the Concord coach. It was a large vehicle, standing about ten feet in the air. The bed of the coach rested on thorough braces, with a front booth for carrying mail and express, and a hind booth, for carrying trunks and heavy baggage. On both sides, near the top of the coach, running along the whole bed of the coach, were rings to which ropes could be attached, so that small articles of express could be tied on top. This carryall of transportation was hauled by four or six horses. These horses were all trained the same as fire horses, and knew their respective places. There were fourteen relays of horses between Superior and St. Paul.

Photo, Minnesota Historical Society

The Stage Route schedule shows the distances between stage stops and gives the usual travel time as 2 1/2 days and the cost as $16 during the later days of the road.

STAGE ROUTE,
Via MILITARY ROAD, running from the CITY OF SUPERIOR, Wis., to ST. PAUL, Minn.—DISTANCES, &c.

Going South.	Miles.	Going North.	Miles
Superior City	0	St. Paul	0
Minnesota State Line	15	Little Canada, P. O.	6
Pine Grove	1—16	Centerville	12—18
Clear Creek	1—17	Wyoming	14—32
Twin Lakes, P. O.	5—22	Sunrise City, P. O.	19—51
Black Hoof	6—28	Rushseba	11—62
Moose Lake	12—40	Chengwatana, P. O.	11—73
Kettle River	17—57	Deer Creek	17—90
Deer Creek	13—70	Kettle River	13—103
Chengwatana, P. O.	17—87	Moose Lake	17—120
Rushseba	11—98	Black Hoof	12—132
Sunrise City, P. O.	11—109	Twin Lakes, P. O.	6—138
Wyoming	19—128	Clear Creek	5—143
Centerville	14—142	Pine Grove	1—144
Little Canada, P. O.	12—154	Wisconsin State Line	1—145
St. Paul	6—160	Superior City	15—160

Usual Time, 2¼ days. Fare, $16.

An excursion of thirty-five dignitaries and officers of the Lake Superior and Mississippi Railroad and family members ("the ladies come to enjoy the balmy air and far-famed scenery of our beautiful state") journeyed from Philadelphia in August of 1869 to Minnesota where they ventured from St. Paul to Duluth on the Military Road. Accompanying the excursion party was John Townsend Trowbridge, an accomplished writer and editor, who wrote a narrative of the trip published in the *Atlantic Monthly* in 1870. His description of the journey on the Military Road just before it was replaced by rail travel, doesn't differ greatly from the descriptions written at opening of the road in the late 1850s:

Through the Woods to Lake Superior

Returning to St. Paul, we fall in with travelers who have fearful tales to tell of the route through the woods to Lake Superior, the next thing in our programme; - coaches mired and upset, limbs dislocated, passengers forced to walk over the worst parts of the road, with mud to their knees, belated in the forest, and devoured by mosquitoes. "Ladies in your party? it is madness! you will never get them through!" We meet others who, after attempting the passage from the other side, abandoned it, and returned down the lake, reaching St. Paul after a long detour by water and by rail. There is only the old Military Road, as it is called, cut through the wilderness for government purposes twenty years ago, and traversed now by a tri-weekly stage. The wet season has converted it into one interminable slough, or mud canal; and it is too closely shut in by over-shadowing trees to be dried much by the sun in the brief intervals betwixt the constantly recurring rains....

...It is near midnight, and it is rainy and very cold, when we tumble from the coaches, weary and hungry and chilled, at Twin Lakes. Two log-cottages receive us, and furnish us most excellent suppers; and we all sleep under roofs this night, some on floors, some on hay in the barns, and a few in beds. Next morning (Sunday, 15th) finds us rested and hilarious. I look about me, and am interested to observe with what cheerfulness men and women accustomed to the luxuries of life accept the discomforts and endure the hardships of days and nights like these....

...The lakes (as we see by daylight in the morning) are mere ponds, one of them full of leeches, which we dip up with the water in pail or basin, when we go to the shore to wash ourselves.

The cottages boast, and justly, of the butter and cream with which they treat their guests. The landlady of one of them tells me her two cows gave her one hundred and six pounds of butter in the month of June last, "and I kept a stopping-place besides, which takes milk and cream." We measure a spear of timothy pulled up by chance in the dooryard, and find it five and a half feet in length; and clover is thick at its roots. Winter wheat, she avers, is a sure crop, yielding from twenty to twenty-five bushels to the acre. These are among the many evidences we have met with all along the route, showing that this vast forest-covered region is one of the richest of the State. Its mighty growths of timber possess an incalculable value for the fuel and lumber with which they will supply rising cities on rivers and lakes, and settlements on the great prairies; and the soil, shorn of it forests, will equal the best in Minnesota, for pasturage, root crops, and wheat....

...We have made this grand portage laboriously in wagons (for the most part), and we have been three days and more about it. The railroad completed, it will be made comfortably in a few hours. This terrible mud-canal navigation through the wilderness will soon be obsolete, and a thing to be wondered at when the new avenue of trade and travel shall be established, with civilization brightly crystallizing in its course.

The current Scott House served as a stage stop and hotel for a short while before the end of the Military Road era, although Twin Lakes had been the location of a station for the entire period the road was used. One can almost hear the horses' galloping hoofs and the creaking of the wheels of the big Concord stages.

Sources
Larsen, Arthur J. *The Development of the Minnesota Road System*. Minnesota Historical Society, St. Paul. 1966.
Luukkonen, Larry. *Between the Waters: Tracing the Northwest Trail From Lake Superior to the Mississippi*, Dovetailed Press, Duluth. 2007.
Primmer, George H. *Pioneer Roads Centering at Duluth*. *Minnesota History* reprint, St. Paul. September, 1935.
Singley, Grover. *Tracing Minnesota's Old Government Roads*. Minnesota Historical Society, St. Paul. 1974.
Superior Chronicle, various papers from 1855-1859.
Van Brunt, Walter. *Duluth and St. Louis County Minnesota: Their Story and People*, vol. 1. The American Historical Society, Chicago and New York. 1921.

"This is a picture of the finish of an epoch. It is the last stage-coach, just preparing to start from Superior for St. Paul, taken September 23, 1871." As quoted from a local newspaper in Van Brunt. Photo, Minnesota Historical Society

MAP
OF THE
GENERAL GOVERNMENT ROADS
IN THE
TERRITORY OF MINNESOTA
SEPTEMBER 1854

The Portions of Roads finished are designated thus ─────────
    do   do not yet completed but under contract thus ─ ─ ─ ─ ─
    do   do remaining to be built & to be put under contract thus ·········

The law of Jan.y 1853 appropriating money for the roads in Minnesota, contemplating the most direct and convenient route from Point Douglas to the Rapids of the St Louis River and not as expressed in the former law requiring the road to run by way of Cottage Grove. The location of the road between Point Douglas and Stillwater should be changed to conform somewhat to the dotted line on the Map. The survey and location of this road has also to be carried on to the mouth of the St Louis River in Wisconsin according to the act of July 1854

AN EXHIBIT OF THE PROGRESS WHICH HAS BEEN MADE IN THE GENERAL GOVERNM.t ROAD OPERATIONS OF THE TERRITORY OF MINNESOTA SEP.t 1854

Designation of Road	Portions finished	Portions under Contract & not yet completed	Name of Contractor	Portions remaining to be built & not yet put under Contract
From Point Douglas to Mouth of St Louis River of Lake Superior, distance to falls 173½ miles	From 21st mile Station to 78th mile Station, 57 Miles. From 49th Stat.n just beyond Rice Creek to 54th Mile Station, nearly 5 Miles Bridge over Rum River, Bridge over Elk River, from 65th Mile Station to 82d Mile, 17 Miles, Bridge over Rock Creek, from 101st Mile Stat.n to 105 Mile Stat.n and from 113th to 115th M.l Stat.n (6 Miles) in all 29 Miles nearly.	From West line City Limits of St Paul to third St. St Anthony a distance of 7¼ miles.	Benjamin Parker	From Point Douglas to 21st mile Station and from 78th m.l Stat.n to St Louis River. From Point Douglas to Stat.n 49 just beyond Rice Creek, from 54th m.l Stat.n (½ a mile beyond Coon Creek) to 65th m.l Stat.n, except Bridge across Rum River & Elk River, from m.l Stat.n 82 to m.l Stat.n 101, except Bridge over Rock Creek, from 105th mile Stat.n to 113th m.l Stat.n & from 115th mile Stat.n to Fort Ripley.
From Point Douglas to Fort Gaines now Fort Ripley 23 + 122½ = 145½ m.l.s				
From Mouth of Swan River to Winnebago agency at Long Prairie 28 miles nearly	Bridge over Swan River, first & sec.d crossings, Bridge & Causeway across Turtle Creek, from third mile Stat.n to 7 mile Stat.n (4 m.) Bridge over Bear Head Creek, Bridge over Swan Creek and from 25th m.l Stat.n to Mississippi River, 3 miles nearly.			From Winnebago Agency to 3d mile Stat.n, except Bridge & Causeway across Turtle Creek, & from 7th mile Stat.n to 25th m.l Stat.n, except Bridge over Bear Head Creek, Swan Creek and Swan River.
From Wabashaw to Mendota, 76½ miles.	Bridge across Hough at Wabashaw with approaches, Bridge across Smith Creek with approaches, from Reeds Landing to Lake Roy, and the grading of the North end of the road at Mendota.			From top of Bluff at Mendota to Stat.n 40 between 70th & 71st m.l Stat.n & from Reeds landing to Wabashaw, except Bridge over Smith's Creek & over Hough at Wabashaw, with the Approaches.

Copied by J.S. Sewall, Civil Engineer.

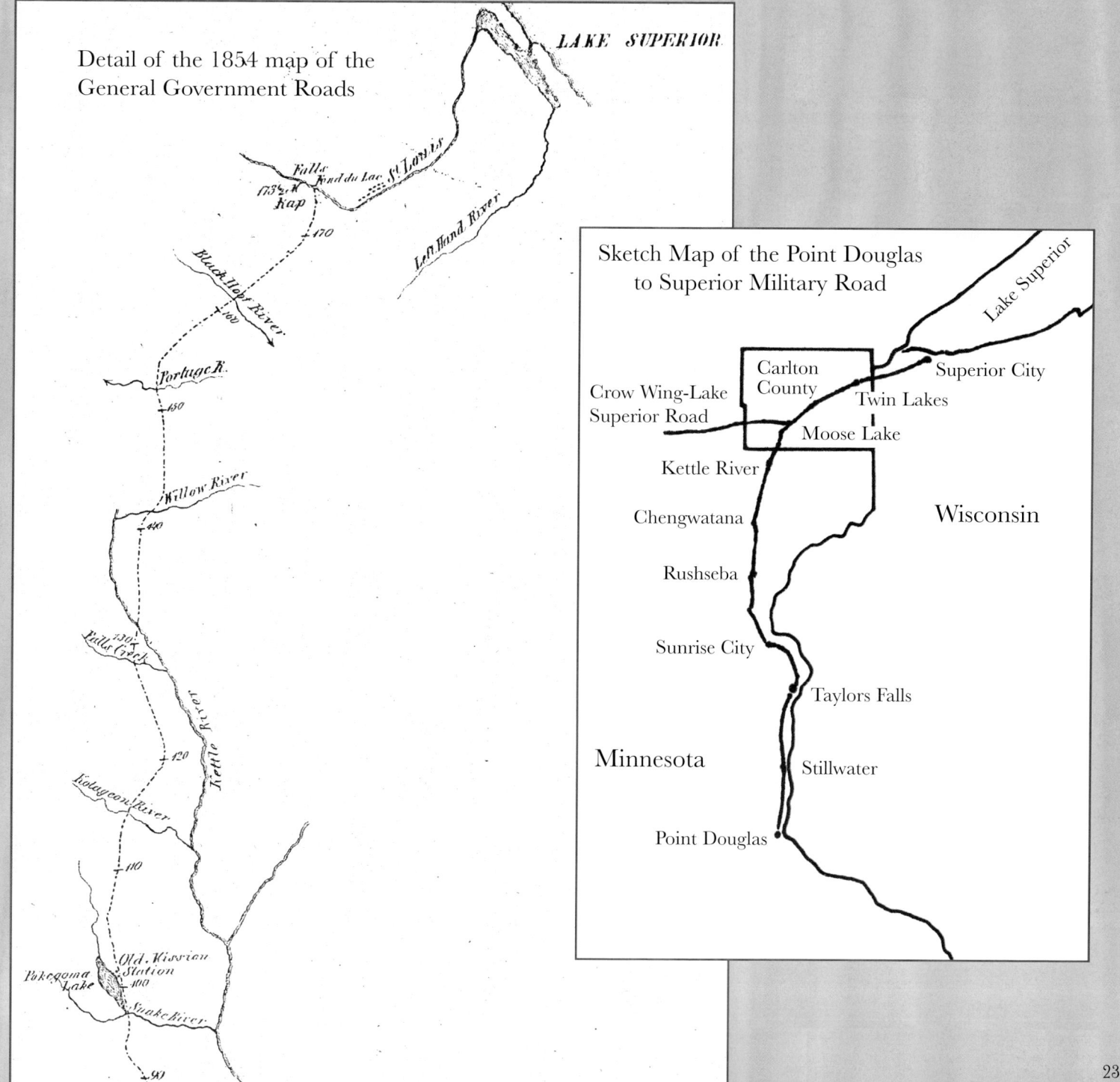

TWIN LAKES
Carlton County, Minnesota
Scale 200 ft. to an inch.

Main Street is 100 feet wide, the angle of Fifth Street is 25° All the other streets are 80 feet wide, parallel with and at right angles from Main Street, Main Street is True East and West to the angle at Sixth, then at 55° West (Magnetic) Blocks are 400 feet long by 300 feet deep, Lots are 40 feet front by 140 feet deep, the lots are numbered from the East side of plat in regular order, the even lots on the North side and the odd Nos. on the South all the way thro' on Main Street and on the other streets up to Sixth Street except South, Linn and Poplar which are No. to Fifth Street: from this the lots are No. to correspond with the Nos. on Main Street, alleys are 20 ft wide.

I, Richard Relf, Surveyor do certify that this map of Twin Lakes is correct according to the surveys made by me under the direction of George E. Nettleton, Edwin C. Becker, George W. Perry, Samuel Cochran and other owners and occupant(s) of Town Site.

Dated Twin Lakes Dec. 12th, 1855   Richard Relf

Territory of Minnesota)
County of St. Louis   )   S. S.

     Be it known that on this 12th day of June A. D. 1856 before me appeared George W. Perry Agent of the proprietors of Twin Lakes, to me known to be such Agent and acknowledged that this Plat is a true and correct Plat of the town of Twin Lakes according to the survey thereof and that the same is set apart as herein shown for the uses and purposes of a town for commercial and other purposes.

                                                                             R. H. Barrett
                                                                             Register of Deeds.

                Office of Register of Deeds
                St. Louis Co. Minn Territory

Received and filed for record at 7 P. M. on the 21st June 1856

                                                                           R. H. Barrett
                                                                             Register of Deeds.

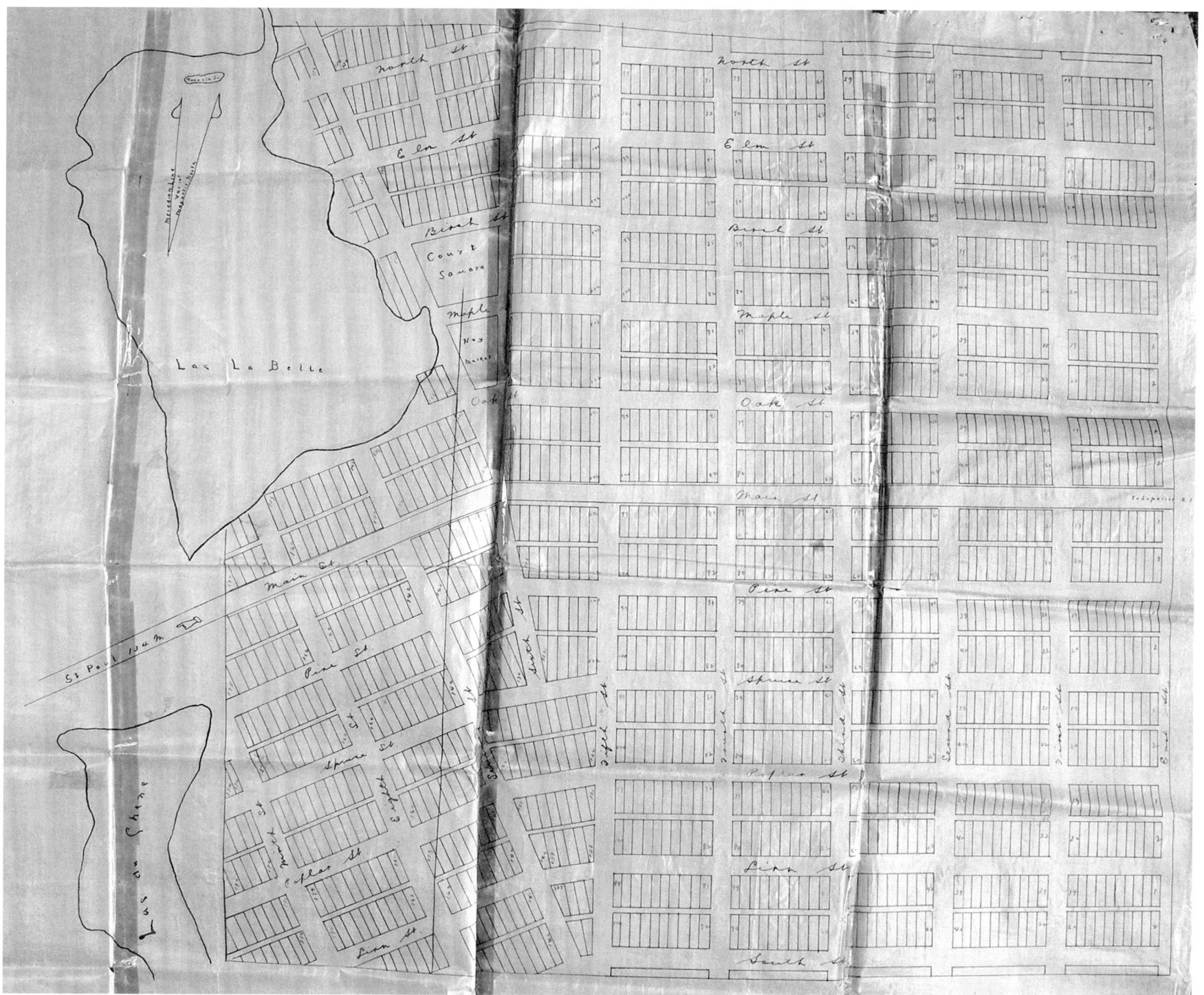

The Mayer Years 1881-1909

In the late 1800s, the railroad companies published booklets of information designed to attract settlers to the lands surrounding the railroads. The booklets were filled with pictures and testimonials of successful farmers which, it was hoped, would entice others to the area.

THE LAND OF PROMISE

FOR FARMERS, DAIRYMEN, STOCK RAISERS, MARKET GARDENERS, ETC.

A BRIEF DESCRIPTION
OF THE
RESOURCES AND POSSIBILITIES
OF THE COUNTRY TRIBUTARY TO THE

SAINT PAUL & DULUTH RAILROAD

AND GENERAL INFORMATION ABOUT
THE STATE OF

MINNESOTA

The Land of Promise was published by the St. Paul & Duluth Railroad Company in 1887. It contained the following article written by Joseph Mayer who, with his wife Rebecca, owned Scott House 1881-1909:

Never Found a Place Like It

Carlton, Minn., July 27, 1895

I have been here for twenty-two years and came here from Superior, Wis. I first bought an eighty-acre tract of land and later on bought 153 acres more adjoining the first piece. I have done general farming but have devoted most of my time and attention to gardening. My crops have never been failures and my garden stuffs have always been of the first quality. My strawberries in particular cannot be excelled anywhere and would find ready sale and high prices in the market, as they are large, firm and finely flavored, but I have never attempted to grow more than I need for the use of my own family.

I was born near Cologne, in Germany, and have traveled very extensively, but I have never found a place that pleased me more than this does, for the climate is very healthful, the soil is rich and productive, our markets are close to us, and the prices that we receive for our produce are very high.

I have a beautiful lake, about fifteen acres in area, of clear, cold water on my farm and have stocked it with several thousand brook trout. In a few years, when they have grown large enough, I will own one of the best private fishing grounds in Minnesota.

Joseph Mayer

Scott House as it appeared during the Mayer years with a large vegetable garden.

The Scotts of Scott's Corner 1910 - 1937

Minnie L. Scott and her son, Fred Scott.

Walter and Minnie Scott purchased the farm in 1910. The purchase included the house (now Scott House), large hay barn and several additional outbuildings. Prior to their moving to Carlton, the Scotts lived in Duluth. Mr. Scott was a purchasing agent for Universal Flour Milling in Duluth. This position had afforded him the opportunity to work as an agent in London, England, in the early 1880s. Probably the most interesting information about the Scotts was the fact that Minnie and Walter A. Scott divorced in 1914. Of course at this time in history divorce was almost unheard of. The Scott descendents were not able to shed much light as to the reason for this parting of union. For years local gossip simply said, "He had a wandering eye for the ladies!" Following their divorce Minnie Scott, along with her sons, Walter T. and Russell, remained on the farm.

Their purchase of the farm brought many improvements to the property. The house was raised and the original cellar was enlarged with a permanent poured rock and mortar foundation added under the house. Central heating was installed at the same time. The original chimneys in the house did not go down as far as the cellar, so a tall poured cement chimney was constructed during the basement excavation process. A large wood-burning furnace was then connected to this chimney. The freestanding chimney was quite unattractive and dominated the south façade of the house; it was pulled down in 1946. My grandparents used this old heating system for a few years and I remember my dad telling me that the furnace would take logs up to four feet long.

The next major improvement was the installation of indoor plumbing. This system was very sophisticated for the time. Underground water piping down to the lake was installed at the time of the basement excavation allowing water to be pumped by a pressure system to a 500 gallon iron tank in the basement. Because the house had no electricity, the pump was operated by a gasoline engine. A bathroom was installed in one of the second floor bedrooms and a cess pit was constructed east of the house. The waste was carried by large glazed sewer pipes made by the Red Wing Pottery Company. This system broke down at some point, and the Scott family lived in the house for many years without plumbing. When my dad was little he would deliver water to Mrs. Scott and in return she would give him fresh cream to take to my grandmother. By the time Mrs. Scott passed away in 1937, the house had fallen into disrepair. The exterior had never been painted and so the very dark, weathered siding gave the home the classic "haunted" look. My mother remembers riding by the house when she was little and she would always cover her eyes when they drove by the "creepy old place!" An interesting discovery when my grandparents bought the house was 24 gallons of exterior house paint tucked away in an unused bedroom upstairs. The central location of Scott House and the beautiful lake offered a lovely spot in the summer for many community and church gatherings. Minnie Scott opened her grounds to many and was considered a very gracious host.

Scott House in the early 1940s with its unpainted exterior and in a state of disrepair.

Walter and Minnie Scott had six children. Until the family returned to see the farm in 2000 they assumed there were only five children. However, on a journey to Forest Hill Cemetery in Duluth, they discovered the grave of an infant daughter who died in 1894. Her name was Minnie. The grandchildren were quite surprised by this discovery as it was never mentioned within the family circles. The surviving children were: Fred, Walter, Mary, Laila, and Russell. Walter and Russell were the only two that actually lived at Scott House. Fred owned 40 acres and a small summer home just opposite Scott's corner. He and his family had planned to retire there, but he died tragically in 1931. Fred was general manager of the Heinz Company in Duluth and one Sunday suffered a fatal fall in an elevator shaft as he was leaving the building.

From the Scott Family Album

A Scott family gathering in 1923. Minnie Scott is standing in the center in the light dress.

Laila Scott Humphreys in Lac La Belle.

A community social gathering at Twin Lakes, ca. 1915.

Off to pick blueberries, ca. 1912.

Mary Scott Bywater with her daughters, Jay and Marian, in the field around 1911.

An outing at Scott House, date unknown.

Russell Scott and his dog pictured with a wolf cub and its dead mother.

An unidentified man carries a frozen deer at Scott House, ca. 1920s.

Lonely and Abandoned

Following the death of Minnie Scott in January, 1937, her bachelor son Walter remained in the house for a time after which the house became empty for several years. My dad remembered going to see Walter one day. It was quite cold and he was living only in the kitchen. He had sealed off the doors to the other rooms with cardboard and on this bitterly cold afternoon, there was Walter, bundled up in an old sheepskin coat with his feet on the kitchen range, reading a western pulp magazine. A short time later he moved to Florence, Wisconsin, to live near his brother Russell and family. He died there in 1956.

Following the probate of Minnie Scott's will, the personal property was removed and sold at auction in Carlton in the spring of 1937. Their fine Victorian furniture was crafted of walnut, cherry, and oak. Several pieces were ornamented with marble tops. There were a few pieces left in the house—a very large cherry dining room table and a two-piece gentlemen's dresser. Unfortunately these pieces were destroyed by my grandfather. However, I was able to track down a large walnut cupboard which had belonged to the Scott family and purchased it at a private estate sale in 2001. The other interesting piece of furniture is the infamous Grandfather Clock. Growing up I often heard my grandparents talk about the Scotts and in these conversations they would mention a grandfather clock. Of course, being a very curious young boy, I was always fascinated by the clock story. My fascination became more intense when I researched the Scott divorce decree and the clock was mentioned. On one of my field trips to Ann Arbor, Michigan, to visit my dear friend Marian Wright (granddaughter of Minnie Scott), I stopped in Iron Mountain, Michigan, to visit Eileen Scott. I had met Eileen along with other family members in 2000 when they visited the farm. Eileen's husband, Russell (Hap) had passed away a few months before. Eileen was quite surprised to see me and welcomed me with open arms. As I entered her living room there before me was a beautiful grandfather clock. It really took my breath away. "That came from the farm," Eileen remarked. That elegant yet simple clock returned to its same spot in the alcove on the "farm" in October 2005 as a generous loan to Scott House by Eileen Scott and her family. I learned later that Eileen's son Tom and his boys had stopped by the farm that previous summer. Unfortunately I was not available to meet them, but one of my staff gave them a tour. After Tom was there he told his mother that the clock needed to go back to the "farm." Also on my visit to see Eileen she gave me two beautiful etchings, circa 1890, that had once hung in Scott House.

The grandfather clock stands once again in the alcove at Scott House.

Minnie Scott's Letters

Minnie Scott kept up a lively correspondence with her daughter and grandchildren during the years she lived at Scott House from 1910 until her death in 1937. She wrote about the everyday life at the farm, the weather, her sewing projects, and gardens. They document the small moments of her life with wit and strong family feelings. We have compiled sections of the letters to give a taste of what life was like at Scott House during Minnie's tenure there.

Here are a few letters in their entirety to give a feeling for her style of writing that was breezy, rambling, and descriptive.

Sunday Morn. 11 o'clock

Dear Mary:
   Just a line to tell your kids are here and sleeping at the rate of 40 knots an hour. Budy seems content-so far, with his new home. He sure is a nice dog. They were so tired when they got here so told them to sleep just as long as they wanted.
   Not an extra nice day so don't know what they will want to do. Leg of lamb and green peas, strawberries and coconut cake. Come on.

                 Love to all
                 Mother

July 15th

Dear Mary,
   Your letter came and glad the heat did not keep you from writing, it has been 105 here, so unheard of you know, for ten days around there and I was in bed most of the time. Poor Walter had his hands full but I can tell you he was pretty faithful. I am afraid the crops will amount to very little and the hay looks so brown now, no rain for so long and such terrible heat, in the alcove it was 90 most of the time, and you know if there is any breeze we generally get it but if rain would only come it would help so much. Have not seen Laila for some time, guess she has all she can do to keep going. Tell Mrs. C. when I come she can fix her supreme dish again it sounded so good. Hope you will have no trouble renting your rooms. It seems you are in a good location and they are nice rooms. I suppose I will know this week if I get old age pension but it won't be over $18.00 a month anyway that will help...

                 Love to all,
                 Mother

July 28th, 1911

Marian 3 yrs.
Dear Little Marian:
Seems to me my little girl has a birthday tomorrow and Grandma sends a big kiss and lots of love and something to make a pretty skirt to wear with that nice pretty dress.

Uncle Walter and I were pretty lonely after you went home, and the old Gobble said where is that little girl. Tell her I won't hurt her, and all those little chickies need you to feed them while the little ducks were so lonely not to have any little girl to chase them.

Tell mamma Aunty Wellers Father just died. That makes four gone since Jan. and I wonder if you got my pillow case tubing. Wish you would let me know.

In haste
Mum

Minnie often wrote about the food she was cooking and how the gardens were doing. She also mentioned her love of beautiful flowers in many letters.

Am cleaning out my pantry. I found near two qts. of fruit-juice, so I made sixteen glasses of jelly.

Sorry I could not be at market with you or at flower show but another time is coming. Am sure the flowers are lovely now.

I too will have blossoms for Easter cactus as well as several geraniums.

My zinnias are just lovely, so many colors and so large. The ones I started in the house have sure done well and every color of petunia. Then our glads are just fine now, then we have a few hollyhocks and sweet-peas, but talk about sweet-peas. I was down to see my dear old Buck yesterday and he gave me two such large bunches, he has them along the fence for quite a ways then he gave me some glads so I am all flowered up...

Well I really am not very comfortable tonight. I had fried onions for supper and then ate about a peck of sliced cucumber, they are so good fresh from the garden, so I think I will excuse myself.

A few lines while my dinner (is) cooking. A boiled one, new cabbage & carrots, onions etc. & hot rolls as I am baking today. Been outside fussing such a long time. Got our tomato plants from Buck, but they are so small I think they will need a lot of care. Have near a hundred and have cut bottoms from tin cans & put over them. Cutworms are bad & then it keeps so cold & wet, had on my overshoes & sweater all morning...Well I can smell my cabbage and I am hungry. Had Breakfast at 6:30 so it makes a long fore noon....

The sun is shining, the little wrens singing & working at their new home in my little green bird house and the lilacs in full bloom and look so pretty....

Think this will be a great year for fruit, our plum trees were so full of bloom also currant & goose berry & now the old apple tree will soon be out. I thot sure it was about dead but Walter cut off so many branches so it is doing fine, and I think we will have lots of strawberries. The yard ones are full of bloom and we have picked so many buds & blooms from the late ones. We have had a nice lot of asparagus & pie plant is so nice now, and say don't mention dandelion greens. I got such a big lot and fussed so to try to get the young tender ones but for all they were just horrid we could not eat them at all....I have some spinach planted I can feed you on and there is lots of grass.

Yesterday was hot. I made a cake & two pies had a roast etc. for dinner so when that was over, I was all in so am afraid you can scarce read this. Well my boarders (her grandchildren) have just come downstairs. One will say they want cream of wheat the other wants milk toast so here goes. Must dress my youngest first.

Walter got me the nicest pail of plums from the pasture and I sat just three hours and peeled enough for nice fruits. Now just finished my jell and have some plum and apple butter on cooking and pickles on the go. Yesterday I fixed a place to plant some Hollyhocks. They should have been in before. They are some Fred had saved. He had a quart jar full and his were beautiful.

I am crazy about the zenias and sure must have them again another year, but am afraid their seeds won't be ripe, so remember. Our glads have been lovely also. Been so cold for the last fortnight tomatoes have been at a standstill such a lot of large green ones, have only had half a doz. ripe ones, but that is more than some others. Our corn is so good just now gave Bud a mess....Buck has given me wonderful big bunches of sweet peas and Nan has taken so many to the cemetery.

We just made an apple pie & some graham ? for dinner and have some awful good cheese. Jessie brot some and Marge a pound, so I am cheesing it. My poinsettia is coming just fine. It is going to be beautiful, and of course the cactus is in bloom.

Very many thanks for my wine. They all say it is the best port they ever tasted and I like it so much. Marge's fruit cake is pretty good with it. and we are going to have your pudding Sunday.

I wish you could smell my kitchen then you would appreciate this letter am making pickles three kinds going, green tomato, cuke chowder & fricalila so you see it is a continual ? to watch things, but I had the things and did not like to see them go to waste. This is sure one glorious morning and I wish Jessie was here to enjoy the wonderful colors in the woods. Just beautiful down by the little lake.

The weather was often a topic in Minnie's letters. Northern Minnesota has extremes of warm and cold which stimulates an endless stream of comments.

This sure is an awful cold morning again, one morning down to twenty six below but seems worse this morning.

We still have snow drifts, but lake is opening slowly. (April 10th)

Such a large flock of geese went sailing by yesterday, too cold for them here.

We sure had a nice Xmas but such a week as the one just passed so cold & stormy. I was glad they got away when they did, driveway was drifted full again and last nite was the first time Walter could get to town since Monday, but we were pretty well fixed for things so were all rite, such lots of snow it ought to raise the lake in the spring.

Such a thunderstorm last nite we could not have the radio on but it sure is a good one yet so many places and so distinct. (November 17th)

We have had such extreme cold, that it has been very little pleasure here, only it has been nice to be together and help keep warm, no trouble to heat the downstairs but when the wind blows it is hard to heat upstairs but we have kept pretty comfortable and the boys are having a grand time sliding. (December 28th)

It is so cold yet the snow can't melt much and yet the roads are pretty muddy no comfort going anywhere. Will be pretty glad to see nice days once more. (April 23rd)

The roads have been so icy. Friday we were down to Fred's for dinner and it seemed the pavement was just a sheet of ice. I can tell you I was thankful when we got home…

For more than a week we have had the most wonderful weather it sure will shorten the winter.

Look at the date carefully. The ground is covered with snow and it is below freezing. How your dad would like that, but just think all my perennials were up so high some showing buds and the fruit trees all in bloom. (May 27th, 1932)

The making and care of clothes and household items were featured in many of the letters.

Hope you can get your dress made. I thot that blue was so pretty. Wish I was where I could come in and help you a little. These days are so short—it is hard to accomplish very much. I am near ready to start on my carpet rags. I need some new rugs very badly. They will all be hit-a-miss but they will be fresh and clean.

I know one thing, I must get busy at my darning. Walter's wool socks seem to give out fast.

Glad you have stockings all mended, now you will not have to lug them all here again, sure a great saving isn't it. I had stockings and pants to mend as well a raft of other things but am getting things straight again, cleaned the blackest windows I ever saw, smoke you know.

I have just finished a very pretty lavender nightdress, makes four new ones, three have not been on.

Jessie says she has made her four dress(es), three house and one like enclosed sample for a little better.

We had a nice xmas. Laila gave me a very nice white slip that will be so nice with my light dress for a change.

Some of the clothes just didn't seem to fit quite right.

The sweater came last nite and sure is a dandy—snug but all right.

It was so nice of you to send the dress and am sorry I must send it back but you know I am so flat in one place and so large in another that nothing ready made comes within nineteen jumps? of a fit. Margaret said she couldn't see how it could be done and look nice, so if you can send material, navy blue, I think it will be best. Am sure it will take five yards, it seems a good deal for you to pay for and I can help out…I presume you have heard from Jessie about her slippers. She was so pleased with them. They were so pretty, but were too tight. I will put them in with my dress and try and get them off tomorrow.

Times were hard during the Great Depression of the 1930s and other difficulties were experienced by family and friends.

Bert is only working about three hours and only has four a week so she feels pretty blue with the rest of us. Both girls have work, but Loyd left so the four are alone.

Now there will not be one thing sent from here xmas and I wish you all to do the same. We can't any of us tell and times may be even worse so for pete's sake hold on to your pennies and show you have a little sense.

It made rather a lonely old house here to take five out at once, but I am used to being alone, and I sure was tired, but I have my big jug of wine as a comfort and solace so many a nip I have before going to bed, makes me sleep anyway, just hope it will last this winter.

Your letter came yesterday and glad to hear from you. Am so glad for Marian. The way things go around here I think you are all very lucky, but some things seem a little brighter for some, but seems the farmer is hit pretty hard, so many are losing their homes. Potatoes at $ .21 a bushel might as well have been left in the ground. The warm weather sure is wonderful for the poor that have to buy fuel. Come on in and have a free dinner with me. Mr. Ferguron gave me a piece of fresh pork, some cab. (cabbage?), carrots, begies, and beets so I am having a boiled dinner free. They wanted to go to Duluth to a movie Sunday so said if Walter would take them the other expense was theirs, so we were there for dinner and supper and bro't home near a weeks supply.

Russ just sent me word he had sent by freight a box of groceries and smoked meats. Banks still closed there, so had no money to send me but said his credit was good, says he can't be happy when he feels we are in need of something, but we have really gotten along very nicely.

I had that spot on my face treated with radium. The Dr. did not like the looks of it, so it makes my face a little sore but not bad.

Other letters were filled with warm accounts of family events and affection for her grandchildren.

Then Nan had us there for dinner & Willa Mae with Maxine and a friend of hers had driven up. You can know Nan had a wonderful dinner. The climax was the birthday cake. You see Carol just got home from camp and her birthday being the fifteenth Nan had the cake for both of us. She out did herself in decorating the cake, white with pink roses, green leaves & stems, then pink candles. Willa Mae looked so nice and we had a nice visit. (August 21st, 1931)

Jerry quite decided he wanted to stay here and take the bus to school in Carlton. I told him he would miss Mother & Daddy so he said all rite I will talk it over with Dad and maybe I will wait till I am older. He went across the lake on snow shoes all around but those little legs got pretty tired.

Thanks very much for my nice long letter and the nice box of candy. They both came Wed. eve & Russ was here so we all had a nice treat - a regular party, as all had been down town and brought a lovely plant to me in full bloom. Jessie could not come over so we had our nice dinner to ourselves & such a good dinner as it was. Sure Russ had good luck. Got two nice deer, one a large buck.

I presume Bee is home or on her way. I too had a card from her, then bless her old heart, here came a nice box of crystalized ginger that was the best I ever tasted. It sure was pretty nice & thick. She did not forget her old Granny.

Well you would not know Scotts Corner on a Sunday afternoon. Our gas station man has turned his extra land over for ball games. The road on each corner was just lined with trucks & cars yesterday. You just wonder where they all come from, sure was a busy place.

Jerry is sure alive wire but he is at the cute age when he is lots of company & Walter & Bob did the work and Jerry and I went for a nap, then the dishwasher went to a ball game so we had a fine old rest. Walter sure likes to have the boys here, they are after him all the time, and the questions that are asked can't be counted. Bob is trying to make a raft. He sure has a great time.

Your tel. came then your nice card. Many thanks for all thoughtfulness. We had a very nice day. Fred phoned me in the morning and said he and Nan were coming out & Nan would bring the dinner and that was pig hocks & sauerkraut with a mince pie to finish. Then a meat loaf & cake for supper, with a nice box of candy & some jonquils from her garden. They are so lovely & bright. After dinner Fred took us for a lovely long ride down around Moose Lake. After supper we had two games of bridge. I wonder if the day could have been much fuller.

Tuesday Dec. 31st—29
Dear Mary:

Your letter came last night telling me of your nice xmas and we sure were glad to get it. It did seem nice to have the phone message. Wonderful when you think of the distance. We were so pleased about the radio, too good to be true.

Minnie Scott with two of her grandchildren.

Well I have just been out and fed my chickens & turkeys. Tell Bob I sure would keep him busy, helping open the boxes of rice flakes. Fred got six wild mallard ducks so they are here to be fed cereal too. They are so nice and will look so pretty on the lake this summer. How many young will there be, one drake among?

You would laugh to see the lambs run & jump & kick their heels together while in the air. They sure are funny things.

It Might Have Been a Golf Course...

For a half a dozen years after Minnie Scott's death, the farm was in a transition period before being purchased by the Sheetz family in 1942. An ad and a news item appeared in the Carlton newspaper in February of that year:

John Duffy, popular owner of a store, filling station and tavern, a few miles south of Carlton, has an ad in this week to sell either part or all of the historic old farm known as Scott's Corner. Most everyone in the county knows this farm, located on big Twin Lake. John tells me that in 1847 it was once considered for the county seat before the county had organized. Incidentally, located on the famous Military road, it was at one time a main stop for the first stage coaches that traveled the dangerous territory from the Twin Cities northward. Twin Lakes was known in the "Injun" days as Lake La Belle. Last year a Cloquet gentleman planned on purchasing the site and building a golf course on it. The scenery is perfect and a good course would attract many customers. However, death put an end to the venture before it started.

Carlton County Vidette, February, 1942.
Note: Twin Lakes did serve as the county seat of Carlton County from 1857-1870.

> FOR SALE—PART OR ALL OF HIStoric old farm known as Scott's Corner. Several buildings included. Situated on shore of Big Twin lake, four and a half miles south of Carlton. Ideal site for golf course, reasonable. Duffy's Store, Wrenshall. 4-P

John Duffy in his World War II uniform.

Scott's Corner store and tavern at the intersection of County Roads 3 & 4. ca. 1940s.

The Sheetz Family at Scott House

My grandparents, Harry and Rowena Sheetz, with my uncle Ron and my dad moved into the Scott House in 1940. They rented the place from John Duffy who used the upper rooms for a brief period. My grandparents purchased the house and property in February 1942 for $3500.00.

Several weeks before my parents were married in May 1946, my dad decided that they would create an apartment in the upstairs of Scott House. My grandparents lived downstairs and had never really used the upper rooms. As Dad put it, "We'll just live there for a short time until we buy a home of our own." They moved out over 50 years later! My mother recalls vividly the anticipation of preparing those rooms for their new abode.

Ron Sheetz at Scott House in the early 1940s.

"It was early spring when Gram and I fixed up three rooms upstairs for Don and me. The rooms had a musty smell about them and it was obvious that it had been a very long time since those rooms had been decorated. The wallpaper was quite faded and there were no curtains at the windows. Still, there was a lovely peacefulness about those large, empty rooms. I can still remember the bright morning sun streaming across those worn floors." It didn't take long to get the apartment in order. Mother and Gram wallpapered each room and put a fresh coat of paint on the doors and trim. Once completed, their "cozy little nest" (as Dad referred to those rooms) included a living room, bedroom and kitchen. They had no running water in the beginning, but Dad eventually installed cold running water up to the kitchen. He devised a make-shift drain for the sink. "The first thing Don bought after our honeymoon was a dipper and pail." The rooms were very cold in the winter and of course quite hot in the summer. The large wood furnace in the basement didn't always provide adequate heat for the second story, so Dad installed an airtight wood heater in the kitchen. "Those heaters were always so dangerous…very thin sheet metal that would almost glow when it got very hot. We were quite happy in those early years; living on very little income."

Throughout the years our family has enjoyed many humorous stories of when my folks were first married. "I was making supper for Don one Saturday, when a man came up the back kitchen stairs. It startled me because those stairs were not being used any longer. I immediately asked the gentlemen what he wanted and he told me to be quiet and then he ran down the front stairs and out across the field." It turned out that the sheriff was on the chase for this man because he was trying to get out of paying alimony.

The house was not very air-tight in the early years. "One August Gram and I decided we would can a lug of bing cherries. We left half the crate until another day and the next morning every cherry was gone! We concluded that a pack rat had carted every one away during the night without a trace." When Joe Malkovich and I removed the plaster ceiling in the lower dining room in 2000, we were showered with hundreds of cherry pits. Dad and I figured that the pack rat had entered this space through a knot hole in the floor in their upper kitchen. There is one more creepy rat tale I must tell. (My dad loved to share this story with us when we were little). "One night Doris and I heard a large crash downstairs. I went right down only to be met by my folks, who also heard the loud crash. We three discovered that our Scottie dog was the proud capturer of a very large rat. Apparently the rat ran up the wall and when it came down Scottie was waiting. The rat measured 18 inches from whiskers to the tip of the tail." In case you are wondering, the rats are long gone!

My parents moved downstairs in 1949 and bought the house at that time from my grandparents for $3,000. My grandparents moved to Mankato and then back to Cloquet to operate the Blue Room Restaurant. They retired in 1954 and built a small home near Scott House. That small house was eventually sold and moved off the property.

Lac La Belle is the larger of the Twin Lakes that provided the name for the surrounding community.

When I was growing up at Scott House there was always activity. The lake and expansive grounds provided a great spot for various family reunions and picnics every summer. It seemed that my grandparents always had relatives from somewhere stopping by for a visit. When I was quite small—cousins, aunts, and uncles began arriving one summer Saturday. They continued arriving at our doorstep until nightfall when the final count for sleeping was 28! Of course our musty, old canvas tent that had been rolled up for years had become home to squirrels and so inside everyone came. "We removed mattresses from beds and slept on the box springs," my dad often recalled. He also added that it was always my mom's side of the family that would show up unexpectedly!

There was always something to do. My brother Tom loved to build things and designed and constructed his own tree house. He also installed a small golf course amidst the trees down by the lake. My brother and sisters were older than I, so I spent many childhood hours with my good chums Daryll and Dale Carlson. I was not as handy with a hammer as my brother, so my dad hired our handy man, Gene Rennquist, to build a tree house for my friends and me. This summer hideaway was nestled in the woods secured to a very old white pine. The lookout stand provided great views of the lake and allowed us to spot any approaching "bandits" trying to invade our treasured space.

My parents were excellent hosts, always accommodating our friends and family. Christmas was an especially nice time with my mother and grandmother working for weeks on baking and various creative projects. Both my brother and I had to have our own tree in our room. I can still recall trudging through the snow with my grandfather when I was five looking for a tree.

My folks always had a tough time keeping me out of the lake. My dad was not a fan of swimming and so he attempted to instill the same fear in us. It didn't work and I'm sure his concern over our being in the lake added a few grey hairs to his head. One day in particular I headed across the lake in my inner tube pretending to be in a lifeboat off the Titanic. I would swim to and from the rubber "lifesaver" when all of a sudden the wind picked up and rapidly took my "boat" far away from my reach. Rather than in the middle of the icy North Atlantic, here I was treading water in the middle of Lac La Belle. By this time my mom had spotted me and was immediately on the waters edge yelling for me to come back. It took a while, but I managed to swim back to shore and Mom. To this day I can still hear her voice echoing across the lake...YIKES!

Mom always managed to find enough blueberries along the lake to make a pie for my dad. My grandmother had a wonderful raspberry patch that we always invaded—out of sight, of course!

Sheetz Family Photos

The "guys" gather in the back yard on Thanksgiving Day, ca. 1942.

Rowena Sheetz with her son Don in 1943.

Don (left) and Ron Sheetz with the '35 Chev at Duffy's Station, Scott's Corner.

Rex takes a dip in Lac La Belle around 1940.

Don and Doris Sheetz with Kathryn Sheetz (Nisula), 1948, pictured in the upstairs apartment.

Cutting wood at Scott House with a portable saw mill, early 1940s.

Don Sheetz sights in his rifle, 1942.

A view of the farm with the small house built by Harry and Rowena Sheetz in 1954 on the far left with Scott House nestled in the pine trees on the right. The small house was moved in 1992.

Tom Sheetz plays on the rocks in Lac La Belle around 1957.

The Sheetz family in 1962. In back—Don, Diana, Kay; in front—Doris, Jim, and Tom.

Diana Sheetz (Carlson) "drives" the family tractor in the mid-1950s. The Scott's Corner store can be seen in the background.

Christmas has always delighted Jim Sheetz. He is pictured in front of the Christmas tree in 1963 and presenting a program on his Christmas collection at Scott House in 2002.

Farming at Scott's Corner

As a market farmer in the 1880s and 1890s, Joseph Mayer was well known for his vegetables and prized strawberries.

Walter and Minnie were not quite as successful as farmers, but never-the-less raised crops and sheep. Their son Walter, who was not considered a very ambitious farmer, attempted to raise potatoes. My grandfather was always amazed that Walter ended up with a decent crop of potatoes. "The fool would never get those damn plants in the ground until almost July!"

Sheep in the snow near the Scott House, ca. 1920s.

My dad gave farming his own personal touch when he purchased 18 cows when he graduated from Wrenshall High School in 1942. He sold them before going into the service. In a letter dated December 24, 1943, Dad wrote, "Because of the added work it made for my folks, I sold my cattle. It made a handsome profit so I am well satisfied."

Don's cows, early 1940s.

A transport truck that has come to pick up cabbages. Harry Sheetz, left, poses with an unidentified truck driver.

My grandparents always had very successful vegetable and flower gardens, but really didn't consider themselves "true farmers." In fact my grandfather worked for US Steel in Morgan Park when they first moved to the Scott farm. However, they did raise cabbage for many years and sold to wholesalers who would come directly to the fields to load. My grandfather also built a large root cellar for cabbage storage. "The first time Don took me out to the farm to meet his folks, Gram was busy cutting cabbage. She was quite embarrassed that her appearance was not appropriate for meeting her future daughter-in-law for the first time." And speaking of the "cabbage patch," my grandfather actually had my dad setting cabbage plants on the day of his wedding—May 4, 1946.

The Renovation of Scott House

After many years of living in an old house and all the maintenance that entailed, my parents decided to build a new home—on one level and basically "maintenance free." My father selected a site on the east side of Lac La Belle which would afford them the best exposure from the sun. As a result he enjoyed six years of beautiful sunsets over our treasured lake. Construction began in the fall of 1999 and they moved in on Good Friday, 2000. Of course I was itching to begin the renovation process of Scott House and by sunset I had already removed carpet and tile in one room. Just prior to my parents moving they received a letter from a dear lady in Ann Arbor, Michigan; a granddaughter of Minnie Scott. Marian Bywater Wright, then 92, and her family arrived on Palm Sunday weekend to see the "farm" and to meet us. It was the beginning of a short, but treasured friendship with Marian. She passed away in 2005. Her keen interest in my renovation of Scott House was invaluable to my work. Her fantastic memory and attention to detail offered many clues to the original layout of the house and some of the changes that her grandparents had made during their time there. Along with house details, she shared many, many stories of holidays and summers at the farm. Her donation of original Scott House letters, written by Minnie Scott, also opened the door to many mundane, but certainly interesting, details of her daily life on the farm.

The walls were striped down to the bare studs, windows removed and replaced, and the wiring redone. Insulation was placed in the walls by Wayne Swanson before they were recovered.

Since I was very small, I was fascinated with the house and its history. I was forever snooping and crawling about the various spaces between the ceilings, searching, no doubt, for clues or some relic from the past. The attic was especially my favorite haunt. I remember one evening when my parents were entertaining guests and strange sounds were heard above their heads. As one guest asked, "Don, do you have mice?"—which we no doubt did. My dad replied, "No, you're probably hearing Jim crawling about the spaces…he is a regular squirrel around the place!" The removal of the false ceilings certainly did provide a very general idea of the original layout of the rooms. So where to start?

In all honesty, I must confess that I didn't have a plan. The whole project just grew rather like Topsy. There were 50 years of various remodeling projects to undo. To my parents credit, they provided a very warm, comfortable home for us as we were growing up. To save heat, my dad lowered ceilings from 9 feet to the standard 8 feet. Modern, energy efficient windows and doors were installed and the kitchen endured at least five makeovers in the years they spent there. My task was to remove the added walls, rooms, and ceilings to reveal the larger, original rooms with their high ceilings and tall windows. It took several months to carefully remove the materials. Much of the dimension lumber was salvaged which required the removal of hundreds of nails. I remember thinking, what have I gotten into here?

My summer worker, Joe Malkovich, then a student at Gustavus, was my right hand man and encourager. He was always very positive and considered any task I assigned him as a challenge. He continued to remind me of the real sense of history this house had. I think it was his positive attitude and humor that kept me going that first long, labor intensive summer. And of course, my mother was always willing to provide Joe with nourishment throughout the day. Joe, with his polite, kind manner, never failed to say, "Thanks, Doris, that was very tasty!"

Stairwells were removed and rebuilt.

Once all the layers of the added changes from the 1950s thru the 1970s were removed, I was finally able to grasp a basic vision of the house as it was originally laid out and how, when fully renovated, could be used as a public center. There were now four rooms on the first floor. The large room that my family had used for our living room for over 50 years was actually the original dining room for the house. This made sense as the room was directly off of the kitchen and there was access to all other rooms on the main floor. The room just off the dining room was known as the "alcove." I learned from the Scott family that this is the room where Minnie Scott spent much of her time reading and sewing. With wonderful southern exposure, this was an ideal spot for Minnie to enjoy many quiet hours in her rocker. This was also the room which was home to the grandfather clock, and there was a telephone in this room. Of course there was no electricity at that time, but the original telephone line that followed the Military Road to St. Paul ran directly in front of the house, so the Scotts enjoyed one of the newly invented devices of the early twentieth century. Another door led into a large room with several windows that we had always assumed was a bedroom, but this lovely space was actually the sitting parlor for the house. The Scott grandchildren had very few memories of this room as they were never allowed in this space. Marian Wright, granddaughter of Minnie Scott, recalls, "We kids were only allowed in this room on special occasions. I remember a writing desk, piano, and a suite of parlor furniture that included a love seat, chair and rocker. They were covered in a very pretty green brocade material." The removal of four layers of flooring in this room revealed the original wide pine flooring. In the renovation process we were able to splice back sections which had been cut out during the many changes. Today the floor is painted an historic, warm caramel color. There is such a beauty to these well-worn floors. One of my favorite views is seeing the sun cast a warm reflection on them. One of the things I hear most from people is the beauty of the old floor boards. So often I hear, "My grandmother had that type of floor in her house." It is so pleasing to me to see the smiles on the faces of guests as those memories come to mind.

The restored butler's pantry.

The dining room, alcove, and front hall have beautiful hardwood maple floors. My dad and I concluded that these floors would not have been installed in the late 1860s, but were probably added by the Scotts. All the other floors in the house are wide plank flooring installed with square nails and the hardwood was installed with round nails. The dining room faces the lake with lovely views. There is a door to the east which leads out to a small porch. The original door in this location had a beautiful etched glass window, which unfortunately disappeared once removed. My grandfather always said there was a porch that had surrounded the back and side of the house. The discovery of an 1895 photo of Scott House confirmed this story, showing a covered summer porch.

A very unusual feature in the dining room is a small butler's pantry which is housed under the front stairs. When added walls were removed you could see the outline of this small closet. The original floor remains intact with the original 1870 faux finish. Stain was applied over the unfinished pine floor and then a graining tool was used to give the effect of wood grain. This process was followed by coating the floor with varnish. My research revealed that all the floors in the house were treated with this process. Unfortunately the other floors had been repainted over time, covering up that beautiful finish. Marian Wright remembers fondly that "sweet little closet under the stairs." "With its glass door it was the spot where my grandmother stored her Haviland china, which she brought back from England and was only put out at special times. She would let me open the door and peek once in awhile. When I started my first job my grandmother sold me these dishes for $100."

Off the dining room there was a long hall which led to the main staircase to the second floor. At the end of this lower hall was a door to the outside porch. My mother said they only used this door in warm weather as the winter winds from the east were very severe.

Of all the rooms in the house, the kitchen has been changed the most. When my grandparents took over ownership of the house, the kitchen, as my dad always said, was "pretty well used up." It was very dark and dingy. There was, however, a large pantry on the south side with a large window. This sunny spot was filled with lots of shelves. Next to the pantry was a curved stairway that led to the upper floor. The removal of this stairway was one of the first demolishing projects completed by my grandfather in 1946.

Dropped ceilings were opened up and the original ceiling heights restored. The line of the dropped ceiling is visible before the walls are taken down to the studs.

Under these stairs there were stairs to the basement. A very crude sink had been installed in a corner of the kitchen and rats had chewed holes in a primitive cupboard on another wall. A large wood cook stove was situated in the northwest corner of the kitchen. A window directly next to the stove, although on the north side of the house, did provide some daylight for cooking. A door to that covered porch, long gone, was on the north side of the kitchen. A very nice decorative feature to the kitchen was an embossed tin ceiling. Sections of this ceiling were salvaged and used decoratively in other areas of the house during the renovation.

Old siding was removed and new lap siding was installed.

Walls and ceilings were restored and period woodwork installed around windows and doors.

The upper rooms always remained in the same layout. The main stairs however were removed in 1953 and relocated in another spot. There were originally four bedrooms and a central room that could be accessed from two different doors, thus making this space an oversized hallway. When the Scotts installed plumbing in the house in 1910, this room became their bathroom. Scott grandchildren also slept in this room during holiday and summer visits. It also served as a kitchen for my parents when they were first married. In 1955 this room and three adjoining rooms were converted into an apartment for a family that worked for my dad. The spaces have now been restored to include three bedrooms and a central sitting room (the previously mentioned bathroom). One of the bedrooms was converted into a large Victorian type bathroom, which includes a very large claw foot tub. There is nothing more inviting than a leisurely soak with wonderful views of Lac La Belle. The original back stairway was also re-installed. Although this did interrupt some large space in the renovated kitchen, the "back" stairs is in constant use by my guests and me.

The Scott family visited to "Celebrate the Farm" on April 15, 2000, just as the renovation process started. Left to right: Scott grandchildren, Virginia Ericson, Marian Wright, Carol Hatcher, and Russell "Hap" Scott.

Guests at the Carlton-Twin Lakes Party sponsored by the Carlton County Historical Society study old photographs. The party was held on June 5, 2000, during the midst of the renovation mess.

The restored back staircase presents a spare, pristine appearance.

Scott House Portfolio

Scott House Recipes

Jim Sheetz and his kindergarten teacher and good friend, Juanita Carlson, bake bread in the renovated kitchen at Scott House.

Countless meals have been prepared and served at Scott House. Its first function was to serve as a way station for weary travelers who must have appreciated a good meal, especially if it featured fresh fruits and vegetables grown on the property and perhaps even some wild game. The following are a few recipes that have been served at Scott House over the years.

Minnie Scott often wrote about menus, cooking, and canning in her letters. Some of her recipes survive and have been passed along.

Minnie Scott's Recipes

MINCEMEAT   Minnie Scott (heritage)

2 cups cooked chopped meat (beef or veal)
3 cups sour apples
2 cups raisins
2 cups currants
1 cup citron
1 cup dried peaches
2 tsp. salt
1 cup suet
2 cups brown sugar
1 cup sweet cider
1 tsp. each cloves, nutmeg, and cinnamon
1 cup beef stock

Simmer for 1 hour and seal in glass jars.

CHEESE STRAWS   Minnie Scott (heritage)

1/4 cup lard
1/2 cup butter
2 cups grated cheese
2 cups flour
1/2 tsp. salt

Mix well; add the cheese, wet with ice water as for piecrust. Roll thin, cut in 1/2 inch strips about 5 inches long. Sprinkle with cheese and bake.

AMBER MARMALAIDE   Minnie Scott (heritage from Jessie)

Shave one orange, one lemon, and one grapefruit rejecting nothing but seeds and cores. Measure the fruit and add to it three times the quantity of water—let stand in earthen dish overnight and the next morning boil for 10 minutes only. Let stand another night, then add, pint for pint, sugar and boil until it jellies. Stir as little as possible during two hours or more of cooking.

Even before Minnie Scott offered hospitality and Amber Marmalaide to her guests; community events were taking place at the house. Here is an account from the *Diamond Jubilee* booklet of the J. M. Paine Memorial Presbyterian Church of Carlton:

One interesting event which took place in the winter of 1891 was a sleigh ride party given by the Aid who went out to the J. B. Mayer residence at Twin Lakes. Henry C. Oldenburg handled the reins, and when almost there very successfully tipped them all out into a deep snow bank. All eatables and everything was spilled, but they managed to rescue most of them and arrived at Mr. Mayer's a little damp physically, but not dampened in spirit. Mr. Oldenburg assured them it was purely accidental, but a number of them had their doubts about it.

Rowena's Recipes

My grandmother Sheetz was a basic, but excellent cook. My mother remembers coming to Scott House when she and my dad were dating and my grandmother was always busy preparing meals for thrashers on the large, kitchen wood stove. These meals (and many of Grandma's Sunday dinners for our family) often included fried chicken, mashed potatoes with milk gravy, fresh cabbage salad, and homemade bread. Dessert was always homemade pie.

Although my grandmother was not in the habit of using measured recipes too often, I have managed to create these very "homespun" recipes from memory for family and guests at Scott House.

FRIED CHICKEN

1 large frying chicken cut up and washed thoroughly. Pat dry. Season well with salt & pepper.
Combine 1 cup of flour, 1 tsp paprika & 1/4 tsp of poultry seasoning.
Melt 4 T of Crisco & 4 T of butter in a large skillet. A pot with higher sides works well for this. You will need to have plenty of paper towels handy. Dredge each piece in the flour/spice mixture and fry until golden brown on each side. Remove from pan and place each piece in a single layer in a large roasting pan. Bake uncovered at 350 for 45 min or until tender.

MILK GRAVY

Use the drippings from frying the chicken for this country favorite. Add about 2 T. of flour to the drippings to make a roux. Slowly add milk and stir constantly. (I use a combination of milk and half-and-half.) Stir until thickened to desired consistency. You may need to add more flour for thicker gravy. Be sure to mix the flour with a little milk to avoid lumps. Season with salt & pepper and serve with mashed potatoes.

FRESH CABBAGE SALAD

Chop up one head of green cabbage. Be sure not to chop too fine. My grandmother used a very large and very SHARP knife. I have great luck with my food processor chopping this. Add a little grated carrot and finely chopped green onion. Toss with equal amounts of oil & white vinegar. Sprinkle 2 T. of sugar over salad and stir. (You may want to add more or less sugar.)

Family Recipes

SPAGETINI Diana Sheetz Carlson

A wonderfully delicious vegetarian pasta dish

1# vermicelli
1 red pepper
1 yellow pepper
4 large shallots, sliced thin
2 cups chopped fresh spinach
1/2 cup fresh basil chopped
1/4 cup minced sun dried tomatoes in oil
1/2 cup shredded Parmesan cheese
1/4 cup olive oil
1 large can of low sodium chicken stock

> I lived in the Scott House for the first 18 years of my life. Among my fondest memories are the wonderful Christmas celebrations we had with close friends of our family every year. Since it was a big house, we had plenty of room to play with all our new toys and games.
>
> Having my family home take on a new life as the Scott House, where so many guests can make new memories, makes me very grateful. Enjoy!
>
> Diana Sheetz Carlson

Prep the peppers by cutting them in quarters and broiling them for 10 minutes until skins are black. Put in a zip lock bag and let them cool. (This helps loosen the skins.) When cool, peel skins off and cut into small pieces.
Pour chicken stock and enough extra water to cook pasta. Save 1/2 cup pasta water before draining pasta.
Sauté shallots and peppers in 1/4 cup olive oil for 10 minutes until shallots are soft.
Add spinach, basil, and sun dried tomatoes and cook until spinach is wilted.
Using a large pasta bowl, toss the cooked pasta with the sautéed vegetables and 1/2 cup Parmesan cheese. Add some of the saved chicken stock as needed to keep pasta moist.
This can be made ahead and reheated. (Great tip–heat the pasta bowl with hot water till ready to use.)
Serve with whole grain baguettes with olive oil on the side and a mixed green salad.
This is a great dish for company.

HOMEMADE FUDGE   Kathryn "Kay" Sheetz Nisula

1 1/2 cups sugar
1/2 cup (scant) Carnation evaporated milk
1 tbsp. butter
1 square Baker's unsweetened baking chocolate
1 tsp. vanilla
chopped nuts

Mix together over low/medium heat until mixture bubbles around the edges of pan. Drop in square of Baker's chocolate. Let chocolate melt; stir and cook until a small spoonful in cold water makes a small ball that holds its shape. Remove from heat and place pan in cold water. Let fudge cool. Add nuts and vanilla. Beat fudge until mixture loses glossiness. Either drop by teaspoonfuls on wax paper or spread in a buttered pan.

HAPPY WEATHERMAN'S CAKE   James Sheetz

1-1/2 cups dates chopped. Put 1-1/2 cups boiling water over dates, cool. Add 1-1/2 tsp soda, 1-1/2 T. cocoa with dates.
Cream 3/4 cup crisco & 1-1/2 cups sugar
3 tsp. vanilla
1-3/4 cup flour
1/2 tsp. salt
Add date mixture to dry ingredients, mix and pour into greased & floured 13 x 9 pan.
Sprinkle with 1-6 oz pkg Nestle's chocolate chips & 1/2 cup chopped walnuts.
Bake 30 min or so at 350°. When cool, sprinkle with powdered sugar.

> I have many wonderful memories of growing up in the Scott House. Often on summer evenings Dad worked late delivering gasoline and motor oil to the farmers, but when he got home before sunset he would always have time to play ball with us. Tom and I built a softball field down by the lake complete with benches and a backstop made out of chicken wire and poles–each painted a different color. We enjoyed so many games and great picnics with the Smerdons and other friends and family. Mom always made her great homemade baked beans. On my birthday in December, family and friends came over; we would skate, sled, and of course have Grandma's homemade birthday cake.
>
> Kathryn "Kay" Sheetz Nisula

BAKED BEANS (Doris Sheetz' recipe) our traditional summer favorite!

1 1/2 pounds Navy beans
1 cup brown sugar
1/4 cup molasses
1 teaspoon mustard
1 tablespoon salt
2 tablespoons catsup
1 onion, chopped
1/2 pound salt pork or slab bacon

Soak beans overnight. Drain beans and add gently packed brown sugar, molasses, mustard, salt, catsup, and onion. Add 1/2 pound salt pork or slab bacon, cut in pieces, and water to cover. Bake for six hours, starting with the oven at 375° until beans are heated through, then reducing the temperature to 325°.

(HARD) PUDDING SAUCE
(Marian Bywater Wright's recipe)

Served over plum pudding, ginger bread, or fruit cake.

1/2 cup butter
3/4 cup light brown sugar
Heat in double boiler.

Add 2 egg yolks, beaten.
Cook until slightly thick—cool.
Add to 1 cup whipped cream.
Add vanilla, brandy, or rum to flavor.

The pantry and shelves at Scott House are filled with wonderful collections of china, ironstone, silver, and glassware. From classic white to subtle patterns on Haviland Limoges china, it's always fun to be creative with these treasured finds to "set" the table for each event at Scott House. Somehow mixing the traditional with my own artistic style puts a smile on guests faces. This eclectic arrangement is often complemented with fresh or dried flowers and greens from the property. Working with guests to create their table settings is one of the tasks I enjoy most at Scott House.

Throughout its 140 year history Scott House has been at the center of community life in Twin Lakes. Its traditions of strong family ties and hospitality have been carried from the earliest owners to the present. Our wish is that many more happy memories will be made in this remarkable place.

Gail Hamre sets a table in the alcove before a Scott House event.

About the Authors

Photo by Kathryn Nordstrom

James Sheetz

is a lifelong resident of Carlton County. He has been an avid collector of history and antiques since childhood. Educated at the University of Minnesota, he holds a degree in choral music education and has directed a variety of musical groups and programs throughout the region including the *James Chorale*. He currently serves as Music Director of the Presbyterian Church of Cloquet, Minnesota, and is the proprietor of Scott House.

Marlene Wisuri

has had careers as a college teacher, artist/photographer, historian, author, and book publisher. Her photographs have appeared in numerous one person and group exhibitions throughout the United States and in Finland and Norway. She is the co-author of several books dealing with immigrant issues, local history, and Ojibwe culture and history. She holds a Master of Fine Arts degree from the University of Massachusetts-Dartmouth and she served as the director of the Carlton County Historical Society in Cloquet, Minnesota, for fourteen years. She lives on the North Shore of Lake Superior near Duluth, Minnesota.